Bygone KIRKCALDY

by

ERIC EUNSON

JUNCTION ROAD, KIRKCALDY.

950

Junction Road, Sinclairtown circa 1908

FIFE HERITAGE SERIES

D1438592

© Copyright 1991 Eric Eunson
First published in the United Kingdom, 1991
By Richard Stenlake, 1 Overdale Street, Langside, Glasgow G42 9PZ
Tel: 041-632-2304

ISBN 1-872074-13-8

The steam coaster "Kirkcaldy" circa 1910.

INTRODUCTION

Settlement at Kirkcaldy began around the natural haven, which forms the nucleus of the present harbour, at the mouth of the East Burn. The date of the town's foundation is unknown, but is believed to be sometime after the 7th century. Equally, the derivation of the name Kirkcaldy is the subject of dispute. In 1710, Fife historian Sibbald came out in favour of an earlier theory that the name means "Kirk of the Culdees" and later writers have frequently quoted him. However, the Culdees (an early Christian sect) have no recorded connection with Kirkcaldy. More likely the origins of the name are Celtic. "Cathair Calden" (town of the Caledonians) and "Cathair Coille Dinait" (town of the wooded den) are two suggestions. The word "Cathair" is pronounced "cair" and the second of these possibilities thus corresponds to early written forms of the name — Kirkaladinit, Kirkalthin, and Kirkaladin. At any rate, in 1075, King Malcolm III gifted the "shire of Kirkaladunt" to the church of Dunfermline. The town at this time is believed to have stretched along the line of the present High Street from the harbour to Kirk Wynd. In 1305, the Abbot and Convent of Dunfermline asked King Edward for permission to hold a weekly market in Kirkcaldy on the grounds that it was "one of the most ancient burghs in Scotland". This right was granted the following year together with that to hold an annual fair at Easter.

In 1451, the Abbot of Dunfermline ceded the burgh, its lands and various rights to the baillies (magistrates) and council of Kirkcaldy while retaining for himself the right to regulate the authority of the baillies. The burgesses (the free merchants and tradesmen) voted on local issues. The laws they passed forbade excessive profits on goods, outbidding each other over property and trading with merchants from outside the town boundaries, these being marked by three ports — wooden gates that were closed at nightfall. These were located at the East and West ends of the High Street and at the head of Kirk Wynd. The town prospered under the new system and by the 16th century it was a major port with large salt works and numerous small collieries.

All was going well until 1559, when French soldiers attacked and then set fire to the town on account of its Protestant sympathies. Then in 1584, there was a further setback when the black plague was brought to the coast by a ship at West Wemyss. It took three months to run its course. Three hundred died in Kirkcaldy.

The 17th century brought more misfortune and disaster. The burgh lost 200 men defending the Covenant at the 1645 Battle of Kilsyth. The civil war also inflicted heavy losses. By the time Cromwell took tribute of Kirkcaldy in 1650, it had already lost 58 ships with 480 lives from its fleet of 100. By 1656, there were only a dozen ships left and within six years the town was so reduced it couldn't even pay the minister. The burgh slipped into debt (carefully computed in 1668 at £3333 six shillings and eight pence sterling).

The 18th century saw a revival in the town's fortunes. Handloom weaving was introduced and a sharp increase in output brought production in 1743 to 316,000 yards of cloth. Leather manufacture began in 1723; shipbuilding in 1738. In 1790, Kirkcaldy got another boost from being on the route of the new turnpike road from Pettycur to Newport on

Tay via Cupar. This road ran along the High Street, ascended the Path, went along Nether Street into present day St. Clair Street and up through Gallatown. It provided the communications that enabled industrial growth for Kirkcaldy and its separate (and at that time rival) neighbours of Linktown, Gallatown, Pathhead and Sinclairtown.

In the 19th century, the industrial revolution took firm hold in Kirkcaldy. This period saw the establishment of potteries, foundries and the whaling industry. A new dock and pier were constructed in 1843 in anticipation of the arrival of the Edinburgh and Northern Railway four years later. In 1847, a canvas manufacturer, Michael Nairn opened Scotland's first floorcloth factory in Nether Street, Pathhead. Sceptics named it "Nairn's Folly", but the laugh was on them — by 1900 this first factory had spawned a vast complex of buildings that stretched from the shore to Victoria Road and Kirkcaldy was the world's largest manufacturer and exporter of linoleum and floorcloth. The industry gave the town its distinctive smell of hot linseed oil that was an unforgettable part of its character until the early 1970s. By 1876, the town of Kirkcaldy and its immediate neighbours had grown so much that there was hardly a space between them. It was decided to extend the boundary, taking in the Dunnikier Road District, Bridgetown, Gallatown, Sinclairtown, Pathhead and Linktown.

A consequence of all this industrial progress and its associated prosperity was the rebuilding of much of Kirkcaldy in the 19th century. By 1900, only in the poorer parts of the town (such as the dock area and the Linktown) were there buildings that dated from before 1750. Redevelopment continued this century with the 1920s slum clearance in Linktown and the 1960s destruction of most of Pathhead, Gallatown, Linktown and the areas on either side of the High Street. The 1960s also spelled the end of many of the town's staple industries. The advent of vinyl floor coverings and cheap man-made carpets led to the death of the linoleum works. In the last decade, the remaining collieries in the area, the Frances and the Seafield, have closed. And yet, despite these blows, Kirkcaldy is recovering. New building continues on many of the "bombed out" areas on the edges of the town; the High Street has only a few empty shops — a few years ago the whole street was scattered with them. Perhaps the new Fife Regional Road will attract commerce and be the impetus for growth in the same way as the then new turnpike road did exactly two centuries earlier.

Eric Eunson, August 1991.

A serious proposal for a steam-powered tramway in Kirkcaldy was made as early as 1882. Suggestions were also put forward that electricity be used to power the cars. In neither case could funds be raised and the schemes were abandoned. In 1897, the Town Council were presented with an alternative proposal — linking a tramway with electric street lighting both using the same power source. In 1899, a bill was put before Parliament for the construction of a tramway, the first part of the system was opened on 28th February 1903. The line ran from Links Street to Gallatown via St. Clair Street. Eight months later, upon the completion of the Victoria Bridge, a second section was added from Junction Road to Whyte's Causeway with a spur to Beveridge Park Gates. The line was finally extended to Dysart in 1911 and by 1914 the Kirkcaldy Corporation Tramway had 26 double-decked cars. After WWI, motor bus operators began setting up in Kirkcaldy. With faster vehicles, more routes and the ability to travel beyond the edges of the town, they quickly developed. After a decade of declining profits, then losses, the tramway closed on 15th May 1931. This 1905 postcard shows the car depot in Oswald Road, Gallatown, which was demolished last year.

Wemyss & District Tramway GALLATOWN TERMINUS.

The Wemyss and District Tramway started operation on August 24th 1906. The line ran from Scoonie Road in Leven to its terminus here, in Rosslyn Street. This picture was taken during the first few days of operation. The Wemyss tramway lasted only a year longer than its Kirkcaldy counterpart and went out of business for the same reasons. This scene looks towards Thornton with the junction of Randolph Road on the right at the house with its gable showing. Nothing remains today of these buildings — most were casualties of road-widening in the 1960s.

6

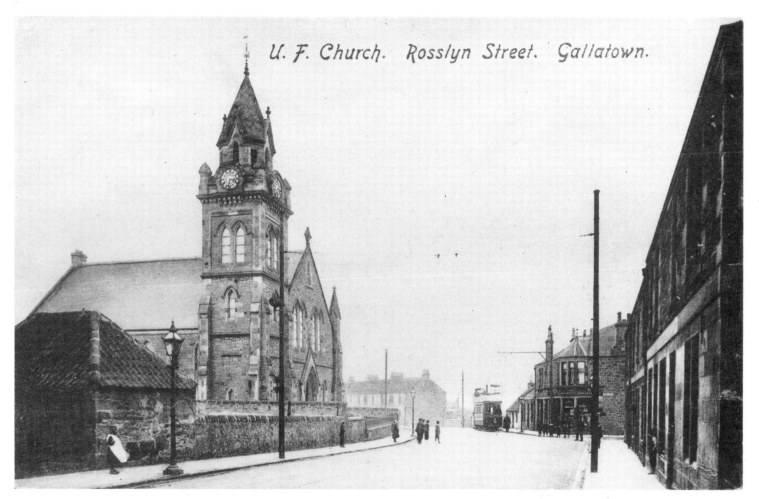

U. F. Church. Rosslyn Street. Gallatown.

The first Free Church in Gallatown was built in 1875. It quickly became too small for the expanding population and was vacated in 1883 when the new church (shown above) was completed. The old building was relegated to be the church hall; later it became the Palladium Cinema. It survives with a truncated facade as a carpet store. Declining populations caused the merger of Gallatown and Sinclairtown Churches in 1977 and Gallatown Church was closed. It was demolished in 1980 and the site is now part of the ice rink car park.

In the early 18th century, the main industry of the village of Gallatown was nailmaking. In 1736, there were 43 nailmakers here. The development of large ironworks, beginning with the Carron Foundry in 1759, brought this industry swiftly to a close. The smiths of Gallatown turned their efforts to handloom weaving and this continued to be the mainstay of the community until the early 19th century. Coinciding with the new road in 1790, potteries were established which continued until the 1930s. When the development of power looms and factory weaving brought disaster to other handloom communities, Gallatown became the centre of the new industry. The first power loom was introduced in 1857 and by 1880 there were nine works in the area. The expansion of the village was rapid and between 1756 and 1801 the population rose from 203 to 1053. This growth continued and by the 1860s the old village had stretched as far as the top of St. Clair Street. None of the buildings seen here in 1905 remain. Kirkcaldy Ice Rink is now on the left.

A Wemyss tram passes up St. Clair Street in 1907. The Wemyss cars were allowed to travel into Kirkcaldy as far as Whyte's Causeway until 1917 in order to prevent congestion at the Gallatown Terminus. The turreted buildings on the right were known as "Kilgour's Buildings". The buildings on the other side of Junction Road were gutted by a fire at a neighbouring cork store in 1905. The walls of the houses and shops survived intact and show no sign of this disaster today. The skyline of this view is now dominated by the multi-storey blocks at Ravenscraig.

ST. CLAIRTOWN RAILWAY STATION, KIRKCALDY.

Seen here in 1905, Sinclairtown Station opened on 20th June 1847 as part of the Edinburgh and Northern Railway. Kirkcaldy Station was opened at the same time. By 1848, this railway linked Leith and Broughty Ferry by a combination of trains and ferries. The line was taken over by the larger North British Railway in 1862. This in turn was taken over in 1923 by the London and North Eastern Railway who operated it until nationalisation in 1948. Beeching's axe fell on Sinclairtown Station in 1968.

The entrance to Sinclairtown Station was moved to this location, on the east side of St. Clair Street, in 1907. After the station closed, the building survived for a number of years, but a part of the frontage is all that remains today. The whole of this side of the street has been threatened with demolition for road-widening for several years, a circumstance that has accelerated the processes of neglect and decay. Many of the buildings threatened are of considerable age, and with a policy of restoration instead of destruction there could be some attractive buildings here. Surely enough of Kirkcaldy's past has been sacrificed to the motorist; after all, what benefit do the people of Kirkcaldy gain from the town being by-passed on every side?

These houses in Overton Road were typical of hundreds that were built between 1850 and 1900 to house the factory workers of a rapidly growing Kirkcaldy. Sadly, many of these streets, like this one with its attractive roundel corners, were swept away by the planners of the 1960s. A waste, for where such streets have been renovated and stone cleaned elsewhere in the town they are attractive sandstone buildings.

Commercial Street, Sinclairtown.

Commercial Street marked the boundary between Pathhead and Sinclairtown. Once known as Back Street or Back O' the Dykes, the new street was laid out around 1870. Most of the buildings in this 1918 photo survive, although the street has been shortened and its Western part has been demolished.

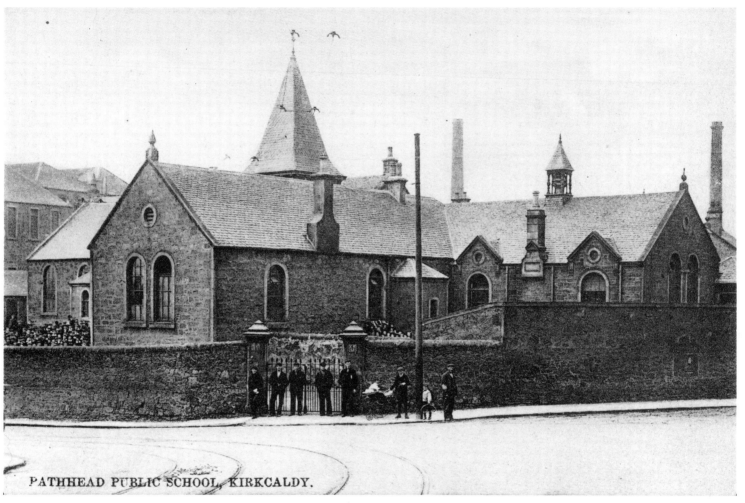

PATHHEAD PUBLIC SCHOOL, KIRKCALDY.

Pathhead Public School was built in 1891 as a replacement for the old Subscription School, and the Philp Trust School in Nether Street. This latter building was absorbed into Nairn's linoleum factory. When these works were being demolished in 1967, it re-emerged briefly with the slates still on the desks where they had been left 86 years earlier! The new Pathhead School has also gone, removed during the wholesale destruction of the area in the early 1960s.

14

MID ST PATHHEAD

Pathhead was an independent Burgh of Barony from the 16th century until it was absorbed along with its annex, Sinclairtown, into Kirkcaldy in 1876. In 1660 it contained 80 houses. Like Gallatown it depended on nailmaking before making the transition into weaving in the late 18th century. From its inception there was a deep rivalry between the Burgh of Pathhead and its neighbour Kirkcaldy. If a burgess of Kirkcaldy bought a house here he was excluded from all his privileges and became an alien. Equally, Merchants from Pathhead were forbidden from bringing goods into Kirkcaldy. This view of Mid Street (or Midgate as it was once known) was taken in 1904. Many of the buildings in the foreground dated from the early 18th century. Nothing remains of Mid Street today. The street was cleared away in the early 1960s and the site is now occupied by the fifteen-storey Ravenscraig tower blocks.

NETHER ST., PATHHEAD.

Nether Street (formerly Nethergate) was obliterated at the same time as Mid Street. The only landmark remaining from this 1904 picture is the St. Clair Tavern. Although antique and potentially picturesque, Pathhead was in a poor state when it was demolished; many of the properties were in an advanced state of decay and had been blackened by a century of neighbouring industry.

16

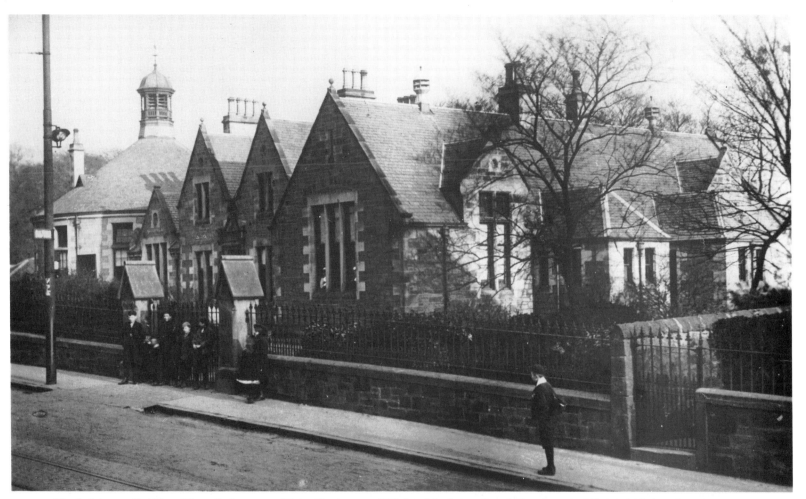

Sinclairtown Cottage Hospital was a gift to the town of Kirkcaldy from the philanthropic Michael Nairn. It was opened in 1890 and originally had ten beds. The round wards were added in 1899. These were the idea of Nairn himself and were based on examples he had seen on his European travels. By 1938, the hospital possessed thirty eight beds. By the time it was closed in 1967 it had become dated and had ceased to be needed with the completion of the Victoria Infirmary. After lying empty for nearly twenty years, it was pulled down in 1985 and flats built on the site.

A panoramic view of Kirkcaldy from the Path around 1900. The buildings in the foreground housed Hutchison's maltings which were established in 1854. This firm still occupy the site, although the pantiled buildings have given way to modern structures. Before this, there was a distillery here which lasted from 1793 to 1841.

18

The Path was improved in 1790, but it was still considered a dangerous road with a steep incline and sharp bends. It was widened in 1876 and again improved in 1902 to accommodate the tramcars. Despite this, during the inaugural run of the trams in 1903 many of the dignitaries on the first cars opted to complete the descent on foot, rejoining their braver companions at the bottom! This difficult bottleneck was straightened and widened in 1965.

As early as 1573 there were twenty three salt pans on the shore at Kirkcaldy. These were owned by Oswald of Dunnikier and fuelled with coal from his collieries. The salt was extracted by evaporating sea water in large, shallow copper pans. The Bucket Patts were a group of rocks which formed a rough square. This provided a reservoir of water to keep the pans supplied at low tide. The salt industry at Kirkcaldy died out earlier than at other places on the coast and was nearly over by the end of the 18th century. In later years "The Patts" were a popular bathing place. They were buried under the sea wall steps in 1922. This photograph dates from around 1908.

20

TYPICAL SCENE AT KIRKCALDY HARBOUR ~ LOADING BALES OF LINOLEUM

How long a harbour has existed here is unknown, but there is a record of the burgh "bigging ane new pier" in 1559. A new dock and pier were begun in 1843. At that time the town was a centre of the whaling industry in the North Atlantic. The pier was wrecked by a storm in 1846. An inner basin was added in 1904, primarily to cope with the increasing export of linoleum. Today the harbour is usually empty, a far cry from this busy scene in the 1930s. Most of the linoleum exported from the harbour came from Nairn's works in Pathhead, hauled in a procession of horse drawn carts down the treacherous descent of The Path.

Both of these postcards date from around 1905. The two buildings on the right with the high gables are the oldest in Kirkcaldy. They date from the early 17th century, although parts are said to be as old as the 15th. Both exhibit street facing gables with crow steps and pan tiles, classic Dutch features that can be seen throughout the east of Fife. Sadly, only one other building (centre) remains in the left hand view. It dates from the 18th century.

The Sailors Walk, Kirkcaldy.

5921. THE SAILONS WALK, KIRKCALDY.

The National Trust began restoring these houses in 1935. Some work was carried out, including the removal of all the old layers of harling, but was suspended upon the outbreak of war four years later. By the time work resumed in the early 1950s, the pair of cottages with the forestairs were roofless and derelict. Although as ancient as their neighbours, the option of facade retention was not a 1950s concept and they were demolished. The restoration of the remaining buildings was completed in 1954.

The Port Brae does not take its name from the harbour, but from the East Port gate to the burgh. St. James' Church (on the right) was built in 1842 but closed in 1972. It was pulled down in 1975 to widen the road. Until 1902, there were houses on both sides of the street and the church was flanked by three-storey tenements. These were compulsorily purchased and torn down to widen the road for the tramway. Every building from Oswald Wynd to St. James' Church was cleared, making five hundred homeless — in the name of municipal progress! Most of the buildings on the left of this 1905 view have also been demolished over the last couple of years. More road widening!

24

SEA WALL STEPS, KIRKCALDY.

The Sea Wall Steps were built as part of the Esplanade in 1922-3. In this early 1930s picture, a large crowd stretches along the wall to watch a concert party perform. The men with the white caps, on the left, are circulating among the crowd to collect money. Right up to the war there were concert parties here and at Pathhead Sands below Ravenscraig. On the far left is the long demolished "Port Brae Cinema".

WHALE 46 FEET LONG STRANDED AT KIRKCALDY FEB. 19TH 1904

Considering Kirkcaldy's reputation as a whaling port, it seems an unlikely place for a whale to make for. However, this unfortunate creature found itself marooned at the West end of the shore on the evening of February 19th 1904. Upon hearing of its arrival, two local men headed for the shore with hedgebills and proceeded to hack the stricken beast to death, in the hope of claiming a share of its salvage value. During the four days it lay on the sands, the corpse attracted hundreds of sightseers. It was finally sold by public auction on the 23rd. There was only one bidder — John Rintoul of Balbridgeburn Manure Works in Dunfermline. He bought the animal for two pounds. Representatives from Edinburgh University asked that the university be given the skeleton and internals of the whale for research. This request was granted, and the skull was buried in a field for two years to clean it!

26

594-88. J.V.

THE PROMENADE, KIRKCALDY.

Before the Esplanade was built, the road along the shore was known as Sands Road. It was little more than a rough track and was only extended to run the whole length of the town in 1860. The Esplanade was built in 1922 to relieve unemployment in the area. It was also hoped that it would prove a tourist attraction and develop the town as a holiday resort, but the elements were not included in this plan and (as every local knows) this is a chilly thoroughfare except on rare days. The tiny saplings in this 1926 picture were short lived and were blown down within a year of planting.

GENERAL VIEW OF THE SEA WALL AND PROMENADE, KIRKCALDY. 5920.

Soon after this photograph was taken in the early 1950s, the grass on the Esplanade was lifted. All dreams of a "Golden Mile" at Kirkcaldy had gone and the promenade was given over to car parking. Over the next thirty years most of the buildings between the Esplanade and High Street were demolished. Although many were of considerable age, most were cheaply built and had housed small industries and their workers. The redevelopment of this area into car parks dominated by massive concrete buildings has done little to enhance it.

28

HIGH STREET, KIRKCALDY.

The High Street looking East in 1905. The Swan Memorial building on the left was opened in 1895 and the upper floors served as the Y.M.C.A. until the early 1950s. The adjacent block contains two pairs of 18th century buildings with their gables facing the street. This was a common feature of houses of this age in the town, but sadly most examples have, like these, now gone.

The ornate pillared shop in the centre of this 1907 postcard was the premises of Barnett & Morton, Ironmongers. This business was over a century old when it was taken over by Arnott's in the early 1970s. Note the pair of griffins on the roof — an easy feature to miss on this now empty building.

An early 1950s view taken a little further east. The "Rialto" cinema on the right later became the "Odeon", but was destroyed by fire in the early 1970s. At the time of writing the white building on the left bears a sign "for redevelopment" and looks destined for demolition.

Thomas Carlyle's House, Kirkcaldy
Thomas Carlyle was appointed headmaster of Kirkcaldy School in the autumn of 1816 and resided here for two years.

When Thomas Carlyle was appointed headmaster at Kirkcaldy he was just twenty one years old. He lodged here, in this 18th century house in Kirk Wynd. According to his writing, he was very fond of the town, but this affection did not extend to his teaching profession and he left the post after only two years. Carlyle was a famous scholar and his biographies of Schiller and Cromwell were much praised in his day, although few people read his work today. Even without the connection, it was thoughtless to destroy this house in one of the town's oldest streets in the 1950s.

HIGH STREET, KIRKCALDY

A.939.

A 1934 view showing the old Town House on the right. It was built in 1826 to replace a building of 1678 in Tolbooth Street and was occupied until the new Town House was completed in 1953. Soon after, it was sold to Marks and Spencer and demolished.

High Street, Kirkcaldy.

The central part of the High Street has suffered from piecemeal demolition which has left a disjointed mixture of old and new buildings. One of the survivors is the old Commercial Bank (1830) (on the right of this 1905 view sporting the awnings).

1100　　　　　　　　　　HIGH STREET. KIRKCALDY.　　　　　IDEAL SERIES.

This 1906 postcard was published by John Davidson and Son, who owned the shop in the left foreground. The years from 1900-1914 were the heyday of the picture postcard, when literally hundreds of millions were sold, sent, and collected annually. In 1903, Davidson printed their first postcards, a series of Kirkcaldy scenes. Within two years the firm was one of the main publishers of cards in Scotland, with a catchment area bounded by Glasgow, Aberdeen and Berwick, and a catalogue of several thousand views. From 1905 all cards bore the "Ideal Series" trademark. Most were printed in Germany as the world printing industry was dominated by that country. Many publishers went out of business at the start of World War I, but Davidsons continued to print their own cards after the links with Germany were severed. The record of central Scotland left by them has been an invaluable source for books like this one, and without them many images of old streets and landmarks would not exist today. The firm continued publishing postcards until after the last war, but sadly all records along with the photographic plates were destroyed some years ago.

FOOT OF WHYTE'S CAUSEWAY, KIRKCALDY.

PRESENT

A pair of 1905 postcards published by Thomas Blyth, Davidson's main local rival. Blyth's shop was located at 69 High Street, and his "Ellenslie Series" postcards numbered dozens of Dysart and Kirkcaldy views. Blyth probably took most of the photographs himself, and the series seems to end around 1910. The older picture in the left hand picture dates from around 1880.

HIGH STREET, KIRKCALDY.

Looking towards the foot of Whyte's Causeway in 1928. The building with the pointed roof was one of the shortest lived on the High Street. It was built around 1895 and demolished in 1937 to make way for Burton's new store. Incidentally, the notice on the lamp post on the left politely asks pedestrians "Please do not spit on the pavement".

HIGH STREET FROM WEST, KIRKCALDY. B.2480.

Burton's art deco building is still a prominent landmark. When this view was taken in 1949 the first floor housed the Plaza Ballroom, while above was the Central Billiard Saloon.

Charles McCluskey poses with his staff outside his shop at the West End of the High Street circa 1910. This shop was one of a group of two-storey, 18th century buildings demolished to make way for the present Presto supermarket building.

WEST END, HIGH STREET, KIRKCALDY.
FROM MILTON ROAD.

Only a couple of buildings at the bottom of the left hand side of the street have survived from this 1905 scene. The photographer was standing outside the present day Abbotshall Hotel. The name "Milton" refers to the old West Mill which was on the Teil Burn. Before the area adopted this name it was known as The Newton.

40

Until Linktown was absorbed into Kirkcaldy in 1876, there was fierce rivalry between the two towns. Linktown of Abbotshall was created a Royal Burgh by Charles I in 1644 and in 1672 was granted the right to hold a weekly market and two annual fairs. A hundred new houses were built in the burgh between 1770-90. The first pottery opened here in 1810 and until 1928 it was renowned for the production of fine white ware. By 1861, there were nine linen mills and four ropeworks in Linktown. Pictures of this part of Kirkcaldy are rare, for by 1900 it comprised a deteriorating collection of old buildings, many of which stretched to the shore in narrow, overcrowded closes. The first slum clearance in the area took place in the mid 1920s and, in 1931, Gladney House (the birthplace of the Adam Brothers) was an unfortunate casualty. It was a fine example of Scottish renaissance architecture, but its location had cost its desirability as a residence. The white house on the right of this 1906 view was the Tolbooth and home of Baron Baillie, the superior of the burgh in the 17th century. It was torn down many years ago during another wave of clearance which removed all the other buildings in the picture.

41

Victoria Road looking East in 1907. The factory on the left housed McIntosh's Victoria Furniture Works which opened around 1892. This building was left empty when the firm moved to new premises in 1970. It was subsequently
taken down and the new D.H.S.S. was built on the site.

The Lifeboat Saturday procession at the junction of Victoria Road and Dunnikier Road on September 22nd 1908. This parade started in Park Road Gallatown and passed via St. Clair Street, along Commercial Street and onto Victoria Road. From there it passed along Dunnikier Road onto the High Street, culminating at Beveridge Park Gates. During the event, to raise funds for lifeboat charity, Newhaven fisher women were allowed free access to the tramcars to collect donations. The two floats in the foreground were from the local fire brigade (note the outstretched net to collect money) and the Haven Restaurant.

43

KIRKCALDY.
Photographed from an Aeroplane.

Kirkcaldy from the air in 1925. The foreground is dominated by the factories of Kirkcaldy's second floorcloth and linoleum company, Barry, Ostlere and Shepherd. From the right, these comprised the Caledonia Works (1874) and the Forth and Abbotshall works (c. 1900). These closed in 1964 and have since been demolished; the site, according to modern local tradition, has become a car park. The wooded area in the centre of the photograph was the garden of Balsusney House. This was the home of John Maxton, which was given to Kirkcaldy as a home for the town's War Memorial.

WAR MEMORIAL AND GROUNDS, KIRKCALDY.
OPENED JUNE 27TH 1925.

John Nairn added to Maxton's gift a sum of money sufficient to demolish the old mansion house and replace it with a modern, custom-built museum. This was completed in 1925 and the art gallery and library building added three years later. Today, the museum contains an excellent collection of local items, including an impressive array of Wemyss Ware. The neighbouring art gallery houses a surprising collection for a town this size, including one of the finest groups of paintings by the Scottish colourists. Both are well worth a visit. Just behind the museum, this photo shows the original 1847 frontage of Kirkcaldy Station. This was replaced with a bland glass and concrete structure in 1964. This too has gone, destroyed by fire and rebuilt in 1991.

Left: Two of Nairn's workers pose with a banner made of floorcloth at the start of the firm's annual outing on July 6th 1907. At the turn of the century Sir Michael B. Nairn organised an annual holiday for his employees, comprising a parade through the town and then a trip to his country estate for food and entertainment. The estate was Rankeillor (the house is now demolished) near Cupar. The workers were transported in specially commissioned trains. At the time of writing, Kirkcaldy Museum is trying to raise funds to restore five of the banners carried in the procession. These banners were unique in two respects; firstly they were painted on floorcloth, and secondly they are in praise of employers!

Right: Davie Dial, a Kirkcaldy "worthy", on a T.G. Blyth postcard of 1906. The only mention of Davie I could find was an old cutting. This confirmed he was a newspaper vendor, and said that he was a member of Inverteil Church. Here, he was noted for the loudness of his singing and occasional vocal support of the minister from the gallery.

Lord Roberts (he's the one in the top hat) at Beveridge Park on September 15th 1906. Roberts was the Commander in Chief of the British army during the Boer War and a prominent personality of his time. He was invited to spend a weekend at Raith House by his friend Provost Munro Ferguson and asked to review some local organisations during his stay. His visit was meant to happen on September 8th and crowds lined the streets to cheer his presence. Two hundred members of the local Boys' Brigade and Cadet Corps stood to attention for more than an hour on a bleak, windy day in Beveridge Park awaiting the honour of being inspected by the great man. Roberts did not arrive, the boys were allowed to stand at ease and messengers were sent to search for his, presumably, stricken motor car. Meanwhile, he was blissfully unaware of the chaos in Kirkcaldy, on a motor tour elsewhere, believing his engagement in the town was the following week! Once he had been contacted and the misunderstanding sorted out, the visit was arranged for the 15th, the date he had believed it to be. The B.B.'s and Cadets turned out again, joined this time by the Fife Volunteers and were duly reviewed. One consolation to the ten thousand who turned out two weeks in a row to catch a glimpse of Roberts was that the weather was pleasanter on the second date.

Watching the band in Beveridge Park in 1910. Michael Beveridge was a linoleum manufacturer and was provost of Kirkcaldy from 1886 until his death in 1890. He left a bequest of £50,000 for the provision of a public park, a public meeting hall and a library. These buildings are now part of the Adam Smith Centre.

Waiting for the Boats to come in. Beveridge Park. Kirkcaldy.

A less talented photographer might have asked the motley trio in the foreground to move on. As it is they add charm to this 1927 view. The little girl must be wearing the most shapeless child's frock ever fashioned. How many mothers today would send an infant out in an improvised pram made of an old wooden cocoa box?

Kirkcaldy Fever Hospital was built as a tuberculosis sanatorium in 1899. The two-storey building in this 1908 picture was the administrative building, later the nurses' home. It still stands today, dwarfed by the new buildings of the Victoria Infirmary of which it is now part.

A 1920s advertising photograph of a lorry body built by Ronaldson's Dunnikier Coachworks. These were situated in the building in Coal Wynd that was until recently the Mother's Pride Bakery. Ronaldson's closed in 1948.

A SELECT BIBLIOGRAPHY

Brotchie, Alan — Fife's Trams and Buses, 1990

Campbell, Rev. J. — Church and Parish of Kirkcaldy 1904

Livingstone, P.K. — History of Kirkcaldy Since 1867

MacBean, L — Kirkcaldy Burgh Records, 1908

Old Statistical Account 1790

New Statistical Account 1840

Third Statistical Account 1945

Kirkcaldy Civic Society Publications:

Links Street
High Street, Port Brae to Bethelfield
Kirkcaldy in a Nutshell
Pathhead
St. Clair Street